Words, Poison and Love

Chelsee BreAnn

Chelsee BreAnn

To the one who thinks things will never get better. To the one in the midst of their healing journey. To the one on the other side with scars that will never be erased.

You are not alone.

Chelsee BreAnn

Words

Chelsee BreAnn

A Glimmer of Hope

You are the bane of my sad existence
My heartbreak every day I am alone
Crushing every bone within my body
Until one day I collapse

You are the fire barely burning inside me
Because every day that I am with you
You throw bursts of sand onto my flame
Until one day, it will no longer burn

But for now, I am still burning
For now, I can still stand
As long as I am able, there is hope
A glimmer of hope in my sad existence

Chelsee BreAnn

Nightmares to Memories

Life is full of nightmares
So I sleep during the day
At night I become one of them
To scare your good dreams away

Pain is a distant relative
That always comes to play
When memories of you come to mind
There's never a delay

I smell you in the autumn air
And on those winter nights
I still feel the warmth of your touch
Memories almost out of sight

But pain turns to bitterness
Bitterness to remorse
In the end, they all turn to memories
The pain still remains, of course

Chelsee BreAnn

A Letter to You

I love you because I have to
Because your body
Brought me into this world
Because without you
I would not have survived
Would not have learned
Would not have grown

But I lived under cruel words
Your hands holding tight
My emotional reins
"Control" the mantra
You lived by
The only rule I ever knew

I love you because I have to
Because my blood
Is the same as yours
But this blood is tainted
And my love is reduced
To the scar I wear
Across my heart

Chelsee BreAnn

Picture Perfect

My life
Picture perfect memories
Of moments not well enjoyed
My Instagram feed filled with
Gleeful smiles and interesting details
Of a life I would much rather
Trade for another

Loneliness and depression
Showing teeth and forming
Just the right words
Because they do not wish
To be caught in their mischief
But the life beneath the disease
Enslaved by insecurities and despair
It longs to be found

Chelsee BreAnn

Words

You do not realize how badly it hurts
When you look at me with love
But shatter me with your words

Like broken glass against my skin
Like a dagger straight through my heart
These are your words to me
And with them, I want no part

But family means more to me
Than you will ever care to know
So I have become accustomed
To dodging arrows from your bow

Chelsee BreAnn

Metaphors and Blood

Metaphors run through me like blood through my veins
Words like breath on my lips
My bones crack with the pain it takes to pen
Such thoughts and emotion
My heart no longer waits for happier times
It expects only to feel pain
But has grown calloused to the feeling
What good are words if no one listens
Emotions if no one understands

Chelsee BreAnn

Pointless

I write . . . and write, and write
But why do I write?
It changes simply nothing!
The pain still hurts the same
Your words still stain my brain
Stinging as I remember every tone
Every word
Every breath taken
For the release of such harsh words
You never really knew me
You never really cared to know
Love without caring
Writing without change
Pretty pointless

Chelsee BreAnn

Glass Heart

My heart
In broken pieces across the sand
Waves rising up like the arm of despair
Scattering forgotten shards
The pain is tolerable
But the helplessness of these frail hands
The inability to fix broken glass
Is worse than any wound
That can be inflicted

Chelsee BreAnn

The Hangman's Noose

Your words are suffocating
A noose around my vulnerable neck
I hang from high branches
Swaying with each lash
Of your cruel tongue

Unable to keep my footing
I choke on the harsh criticism
You've stuffed down my throat
Since the moment my lungs
Struggled to breath

You Don't Care

You don't understand
My heart aches to hear you disagree
With my every word
As you tell me I'm all wrong

You don't listen
Every word that I say is twisted
Into something it never was
Something I never said

You don't trust me
Even though every lesson you ever taught me
Is implanted in my mind
But still, you treat me like a child

I want freedom
Not freedom to leave and never come back
But freedom to come and go as I please
Because I still love you

Even though it hurts
Even though no matter who or what I become
You will never accept me
I will still come back

Chelsee BreAnn

You love me
You want the very best for me
You always have
But at what cost?

The cost of happiness?
The cost of a relationship?
The cost of trust?

You don't care
If you trace the problem back to its roots
That's what you'll find
You don't care

Chelsee BreAnn

Primrose Promises

I met you in the garden
Halfway between
Love and insanity
Bruises marking the tissue
Fluttering beneath my chest
A floral perfume
Masking the stench
Of an all too present past
Primrose promises
Withered beneath
A blinding sun
Photosynthesis
Necessary for life
But everything dies
When smothered
By too much

Chelsee BreAnn

Only the Rain Knows

Raindrops seeping through the window
Tears seeping through tired eyes
Sitting, weeping in the darkness
Flashes of lightning revealing truths
Heavy rain muffling sounds
A build-up of sadness finally released
Only to come again, tomorrow

Chelsee BreAnn

Who Am I

You taught me to keep secrets
To hide away the peculiar parts
The things no one speaks about
The things that deep down
Make us who we are

So I hid my taste in music
My love for erotic books
My body
(It's not like we all have them)
My kinks and fantasies

I hid my fingers
Under my blanket each night
My sinful trembling legs
That only wanted
A lover's touch

I hid poem after poem
Because if anyone had read them
They would find all my hidden secrets
And God forbid anyone find out
Who I really am

Mirror

I've often wondered what it's like
On the other side of the glass
So peaceful
So tranquil
But would that moment last?

If I stepped onto the other side
Would I be alone in there?
Or would I
Be followed
By others seeming to care?

If I stepped onto the other side
Would motion cease to exist?
Unless I
On the former side
Began, myself, to twist?

But if I stepped onto the other side
Would there be two of me?
Would I meet
And promptly greet
Myself in courtesy?

Chelsee BreAnn

I've often wondered what it's like
To step onto the other side
But I think I'll stick
With my present situation
And in my own room abide

Chelsee BreAnn

Rose-Colored Lens

I see the world
Through a cracked rose-colored lens
It is both painful and beautiful

Chelsee BreAnn

Arrogant Waves

Our sorrows ride on the ocean waves
They rise and fall with the tide
The arrogancy of the ocean's gaze
As it's waves crash to our demise
I wonder, could my heart ride atop the waves
And crash into the shoreline?
Maybe then I will feel no more pain
Just hollow inside

Chelsee BreAnn

Nothing

Somehow I am falling
Into the abyss
Deeper and deeper
Falling into darkness
Nothing
There is nothing here
And yet somehow
My mind finds peace
In this empty nothing

Chelsee BreAnn

So Many Days

Today,
Like so many others
I feel as though I cannot go on
I cannot get out of bed
Even though I have been up for hours
I cannot complete my tasks
Even though items have been checked off a list
Walking through the motions
In an out of body experience
Smiling at strangers
Who I've known for years
Contemplating life
While not thinking anything at all
Doing what is necessary
And yet falling so behind
Today,
Like so many others,
I feel I have failed
But I smile so no one knows

Chelsee BreAnn

A Tree in My Garden

I feel hollow inside
Like nothing can fill me
I'm reaching out to you now
Because at one time you healed me

A lonely tree in the garden
Of my insecurities
Surrounded by the life
Of things that killed me

Looking for love
With roots running deep
All I find is disappointment
Disappointment in me

"When will I be enough?"
Asks the willow tree
Limbs wagging in the wind
"Whatever will be, will be"

"Close the garden gates
And leave me in peace
With my vices and vacancy
. . . I wish you wouldn't leave"

Chelsee BreAnn

Up At Night

Like a snake hissing before it strikes
These thoughts keep me up at night

Behind heavy eyelids that long for sleep
Is your snake-like jaw devouring me

Each word tearing at my flesh
Fangs with a predator's reflex

And I the prey asleep in bed
With one eye open full of dread

Chelsee BreAnn

Unforgotten

A broken record
The same notes
Playing over
And over again

Painful memories
Unforgotten
Playing over
And over again

Chelsee BreAnn

A Dying Bird

Your words hit me like an arrow
I lay bleeding on the floor
As you hover over me with disappointment
Judging each decision
As if it was yours to make
No longer a child
Yet treated as such
My wings have been clipped
To your approval
Me, a dying bird
And you, the hunter

Chelsee BreAnn

Exorcism

An exorcism
Hands laid upon me
Incense burning
Cleansing the air

I breath deeply
Waiting to be rid
Of the traces you left
In my mind

I've been haunted
By your memory
For too long
My mind now cleared
Of you

New life
I walk as a woman
Now free
From your burden
Alive

Chelsee BreAnn

Freedom

When will this cycle end?
When will I feel whole again?
You have taken much of me
Turning it into something I cannot be
My body rejecting the parts you've returned
So little of me left as I burn
Down! the bridge you take to my door
Down! the silence that will be no more
I will speak up for myself, now
I will not be silent, I no longer know how
Today, I will fight for my right to be me
Today, I will set myself free

Chelsee BreAnn

Poison

Pain

Thank you for the sun
And for the rain
For the ability to feel
Even though there's mostly pain
Thank you for the stream
That flows so sadly down
To be lost in deeper waters
When no one is around
A reminder to us all
In this world, we aren't alone
Pain is all around us
And has called this world its home

Chelsee BreAnn

A Flower

A flower
Quickly fading but never opened
Torn apart by circumstances surrounding it
Creatures of habit tearing petals and creating wounds

Gentle hands
A warm touch by trembling fingers
Hurting hearts repair each other in time

A slow bloom
Slowly opening up
Allowing beauty to show forth
But with beauty always comes exposure

And even though it hurts, it's freeing
Even though it stings, it's exhilarating
Even though the floral walls have become so accustomed
The newfound freedom and exposure is both beautiful and terrible

To open up
Not to hide within the safety of petals
But to live life to its fullest
Being cautious only when you are not around

The Many Personalities of a Friend

The way you look at me
The way your heart shines
Through the window of your eyes
Telling me how much you care
Unable to hide beneath those blue eyes

I'm not in love with you
Although, sometimes my heart seems to forget
And I pray to God every night
That I will find someone like you

The way you annoy me
Rather, the way you try
But knowing that you think of me
Gives me a comfort I store in my pocket
And take out when I need it

I don't think of you as a brother
Although, sometimes I open up to you
And for a moment my life
Becomes an unlocked diary

The way you make me feel safe
As if the demons of loneliness and fear
Can never harm me when I am with you
Because you chase them back under my bed
Where they belong

You're not a father
Although, sometimes I hide behind you
And hold tightly to what I believe with my whole heart
Will save me from the monsters and the storms

You aren't a lover, a brother, or a father
You are my friend

Okay

When I ask if you're okay
What I'm really saying is I'm not
And I miss you

Chelsee BreAnn

Changes

It's funny how things change
Like the first time I met you
I hated every thought of you in my life

Then we became friends
And the thought of ever losing you
Pierced like a thousand swords in my back

A little more than friends
And all I wanted was to be with you
But I was too afraid to let you know how I felt

Now, being almost lovers,
I find you are the first thing on my mind each morning
And the last when I fall asleep

I hope the future finds us
Safely wrapped in each others' arms
Because there is no place in this world I'd rather be

Hopeless

A hopeless romantic
I'm hopeless for you
You say you are bad for me
But that isn't true
My heart, the deepest shade of red
In my mind, the deepest shade of you
I breathe heavy sighs of dread
At the thought of ever losing you

Chelsee BreAnn

Prince Charming

You're too good to be true
But I'll take it while it lasts

Chelsee BreAnn

Me and You

Why can't I get you out of my head?
You're like a song I can only remember the chorus to
So I sing it over and over
Hoping to find the missing words
I lie naked in my bed unable to sleep
Because you aren't right here beside me

A one night stand turned into two
Turned into three
Turned into you and me
Wondering what we are, what label best defines us
Why label something so raw and new?
Why can't it just be me and you?

Chelsee BreAnn

Overthinking

Thoughts flying through my head
Like strobe light flashes on a screen
I am alone
I am not wanted
I am not likable
You do not want me
Because you have not called me
Because I am too needy

Reassurance spilling from a mouth
Whose mind is overheating
I am not alone
I am wanted
I am likable
You do want me
You're just busy
And I am needy
But that's okay

Goodnight

When "goodnight" means "I love you"
And you are not here
Your absence leaves a cold empty room in my heart

Chelsee BreAnn

The Key to Memories

When songs become keys
To unlocking memories
But I am only reminded of you
Lyrics shaped in such a way
There is nothing more I can do
But let my mind softly drift away
Somewhere lost and far
Sailing the oceans
Drifting on waves
To wherever you are

Tattoo

I want to feel
Something
Anything
Other than the
Anxiousness
Inside of me

A tattoo needle
Dulling the pain
The comforting
Pungent
Smell of ink
The clattering noise of metal
Surrounding me
Like a weighted blanket

I watch as red
Seeps from my skin
Mixing with the art
Etched into my body
Hoping the
Obsessive thoughts
Will be wiped away
With my blood

Chelsee BreAnn

My mind is now
Blissfully dulled
Like a shot of whiskey
With a bite
That crawls up my skin
A vicious snake
I am drunk
On its poison

An Unrealistic Love

Kissing you feels like freedom
Like the stars are not attached to the sky
Like the diamonds in your sparkling blue eyes

Kissing you tastes like passion
A passion never meant for the sane
A passion for the moments unexplained

Kissing you smells like poison
A poison never meant to pass our lips
But a poison neither of us can resist

Kissing you looks like Heaven
An unrealistic vision of the future
Because the world knows we don't belong together

Chelsee BreAnn

Scared

I'm scared of my heart
The way it bursts when I am with you
I'm scared of the dark
The emptiness without you

I'm scared of your eyes
The way they penetrate my skin
The way they never try to hide
The feelings deep within

I'm scared of the world
That will never let us in
How our lives have unfurled
But we never seem to win

I'm scared most of all
Of losing you, somehow
Like the leaves and the Fall
We only have them now

Chelsee BreAnn

Lover's Hues

My nails are red
My eyes are blue
I'm in love with someone
That someone is you

My heart is cracked
But my love is still true
I paint my nails red
Because of you

As red as the blood
I feel flowing inside
As red as my love
That you tried to make die

As red as my hair
As red as my pride
As red as your lust
I see burning inside

And blue are my eyes
Softly searching your skin
And blue is your heart
Inviting me in

Cheshire Love

The moon smiles at me
With that Cheshire smile
One I haven't seen for a while
Who do you smile for, my love?
Because it isn't me

Chelsee BreAnn

Pure Calamity

Your kiss tastes like nicotine
Replacing tears that are unseen
Addiction, a relief in itself
The smell of alcohol on your breath

My fingers walking down your chest
Your heart so broken underneath this mess
My own heart I would gladly give
To see you happy once again

Our ruptured hearts, our souls to sell
A sorrow no one else can tell
Just take a chance, I'll set you free
We'll fix this pure calamity

Chelsee BreAnn

A Portrait of You

I know you
I know your vices and your demons
I know your weaknesses and your strengths
Your heart, your loves, your lusts
Everything that turns you on
And everything that you will never let go of
A mesh of true deep colors with abstract pieces
Putting you together is like rugged puzzle pieces
But when the picture is complete
The beauty
The animal
The complexity
And simplicity
It is more beautiful than could ever be imagined
Patience and love are all you need
And to see yourself through the eyes of another

Chelsee BreAnn

Demons

I wish I could take away the demons
That haunt you in your sleep

Chelsee BreAnn

The Waiting Game

I have it bad
A sickness of the heart
My mind grows mad
As if it wants no part
Knowing well
It cannot end but badly
Even still
I wait it out so sadly

Chelsee BreAnn

Conflicted

You are my deepest heartbreak
My most prominent wound
But every breath that I breathe
I breathe because of you
No matter what the conflict
No matter what the rue
At any given moment
My heart will die for you
You taught me how to live
You showed me what is true
But I don't know how to tell you
I love you

Chelsee BreAnn

Silence's Touch

The touch of silence
The way it feels against my skin
On my naked body as I lay in bed
Alone again

Never enough
For those who say they are in love
But leave me stranded with the emptiness
Of my own mind

People say
That I am beautiful and yet
My mind cannot comprehend
Their words as truth

For who am I?
A beautiful portrait in their eyes
No one dares to look inside
And see
Who I really am

Chelsee BreAnn

Silence in the Rain

My heart is utterly stricken
With feelings I can't quite contain
It bleeds under the pressure
Of which, I am ashamed
For you have another lover
And I've never felt such pain
My jealous heart cannot have you
So I sit silent in the rain

Chelsee BreAnn

Crystal Tears on Rosy Cheeks

Crystal tears falling
On rosy cheeks
The wisp of words
Clinging to swollen lips
Forbidden and hanging
In the air between them
"I love you" never spoken
But heard all the same

Chelsee BreAnn

Freedom Calling

The sky calls my name in ways that you never did

The Ocean

The ocean, it mocks me
As I lie here crying over you
It has not one lover,
But takes as many as it will choose

Snatching them from the shoreline
They have no choice of their own
You made your choice
Now I am forced
To remain here all alone

My salty tears fall to the ground
And are lapped up by the waves
The ocean laughs in mockery
With my life in its gaze

To you, my life will go on
Like the giggles of the tide,
But the ocean cannot let me forget
The night part of me died

You say my life's ahead of me
Like the ships that sail afar,
But you are in the same boat as I,
Our doors still left ajar

Not letting go of the past
Our compass pointing back
We both want our love to last
The currents stop us in our tracks

The ocean, she's a mighty thing
A soft shriek squeal she makes
The choice was yours,
But now it's not
The ocean only takes

Chelsee BreAnn

Dear Lover

My Love,
When I told you I loved you,
I meant it for life
Not just until
You decided to leave me

Chelsee BreAnn

Ocean Eyes

I see you in the way
The waves crash into the shore
Drowning in your ocean eyes
Like a memory I cannot let go of
I gulp breaths of air
As tactile memories
Flood my mind
The wind whispers of a past
That slips through my fingers
Like sand leaving behind
Its gritty remains
I cannot be rid of it
But it will not let me hold on

Grateful

You brought me out of a dark place
Just to put me in another
But oddly enough
I am grateful

Beauty Is

Beauty is broken
Beauty is pain
We become who we are in this beautiful way
Beauty is heartache
Sometimes it stains
We become who we are from such beautiful pain
One day we'll find it
One day we'll see
That there's beauty in everything
And there's beauty in you and me

Chelsee BreAnn

Permission

When did you ask permission
To rip my heart from my chest
Leaving me empty
Without you

Chelsee BreAnn

Imperfect Love

I miss you
I know you weren't right for me
I know we weren't meant to be
But I still miss your touch
The way you thought of the world
The way you loved when I was close
But I mostly miss your smile
And the way you looked into my eyes
So intently until you couldn't help but smile
I loved that
I loved you
But it just didn't work

Chelsee BreAnn

Love's Demands

It's been some time
But pieces of my heart still break in your hands
I forever think of when it all began
Destruction came in the form of quicksand
Sucking us in
Making demands

Alone

Sometimes I feel
I am better off alone
No one can hurt me
That way

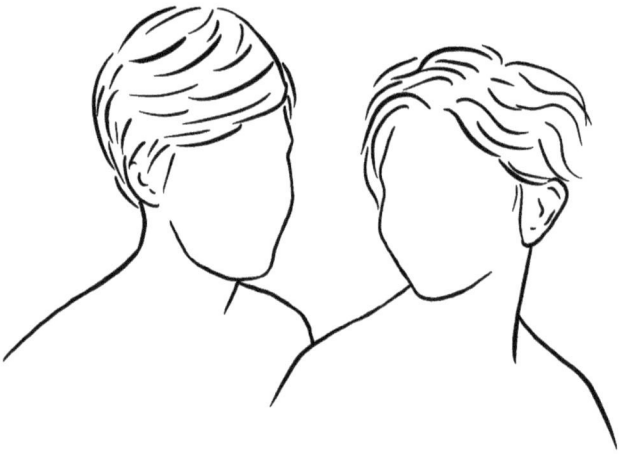

First Love

A love so new
As precious as a newborn baby
Just learning to smile
Just learning to laugh
Just learning what love is
We never thought of how it may not last
Not in the beginning, at least
It was just us against the world
To coin a phrase
It was as if no other person existed
Then reality set in
We grew apart, yet somehow closer
I guess absence does make the heart grow fonder
(Another phrase)
And then finally, the distance was too great
But the fondness never left
It lingers still

Chelsee BreAnn

An Eternity of Sadness

Our love was never like
A warm summer night
Under shyly smiling stars

It was never like a tsunami
Wild and exciting
Before destroying everything

It was more like a thunderstorm
With our thunderous moments
All ending the same way
Like the constant pitter-patter of rain
Causing what felt like an eternity of sadness

The End of the Saddest Love Story Ever Written

In my mind, you were everything
My heart
My life
My soul
Every word that was written
The subject of each poem
Until one day I realized
If those poems were bound
They would be the saddest love story ever written

Regrets

I should never have tried
To heal myself
With your love

I should have known
It was tainted
From the beginning

Bloom

I wrote my heart
Words on the page
Written in blood
And empty tears
A long journey
Through past and present
Manifesting
A lively future
These dead vines
Running through my veins
Will bloom again
Vivid and thriving
My pen scrawls
On empty pages
Willing the future
Into existence
As I watch it unfold

Love

Chelsee BreAnn

A Vow

You are mine
And I am yours
Forever
No matter what our past
The future only holds
Images of us
I run from my past
Into your arms
Not running from the truth
But running from what once was
And no longer is

Chelsee BreAnn

Hold me

I love the way you hold me
As if time itself has stopped in its tracks
And has left us in this one sweet moment
Forever

Listening to your heart beat softly
My head against your chest
Feeling the irregular beat of your heart
I wonder if it hurts

I do not dare start a ripple
In the stagnant time
That I longingly wish would never end

You rest your head on mine
Because the contact that our bodies have made
Does not satisfy your need to be near me

But as the night lies still around us
The silence is finally broken
And we are forced to say "good night"

Lonely Dreams

It's like you are a dream
A vivid vision of the perfect person
Holding me every night
And kissing me in the morning
But when I go about my day,
I wonder if you are real
Or if you appear in my dreams
Because my heart has been lonely
For too long

Chelsee BreAnn

Being with You

With you
I love
Just simply
Being

Chelsee BreAnn

Free

Free from burden
Free from shame
Free to be
And free to tame
Beast inside
Or set her free
Free awakening
Freely me

Chelsee BreAnn

How to Treat a Woman

You're as refreshing as a cool pond
Still chilled from a harsh winter
On an early summer's day
The way your words are full of honesty
And your actions of respect

Chelsee BreAnn

Love at First Sight

If ever I believed
In love at first sight
That moment would be now
With you

Chelsee BreAnn

More

The smell of your lust
I wait powerless
Our clothes strewn across the floor
Your soft, warm lips
All over my skin
Always leaving me wanting more

Your Kiss

When I kiss you
I sprout wings like an eagle
And fly above the world with a conquering hand

When I kiss you
My heart's sadness disappears
And I become the demon of passion lurking inside

When I kiss you
I am the woman who knows she is beautiful
And the innocent not knowing what is to come

When I kiss you
The earth spins all the more
And my heart seems to burst with love for you

Your Touch

Just a touch
And you send my heart racing
Just a smile
And you melt my heart, too
Just a glance
And I know you're thinking of me
Just a touch
And I know you love me, too

Gravity

We are the stars
Once lost and now found
Only to get lost again in each other's eyes
Every single time our eyes meet
I am guided by your light
I am strengthened by your love
Drawn to you like a firefly to the night
Unable to escape your gravity

Chelsee BreAnn

My World

My whole world
From now until forever
You are

Touch Me

Like a shot of whiskey on the coldest of nights
. . . More like shots of whiskey as my body shivers
First, because of the cold
Second, because of the whiskey
And last, because of your touch
Touch me again

Chelsee BreAnn

The Sound of Rain

The hypnotic sound of raindrops
Constantly hitting the sidewalk
As I lay inside waiting for you
Who knows what adventures await us
After your arrival

Chelsee BreAnn

In Bed with You

I can't wait to lay in bed with you and cuddle
While listening to the soft splashes
Of raindrops outside our window

Chelsee BreAnn

Sunshine

You're like the sunshine
Bright
Spreading positivity and helping things to grow

Chelsee BreAnn

Together

I became new
When I found you
No longer broken
But whole
Together
We are whole

Chelsee BreAnn

Thinking of Me

Thank you
For helping me heal
Even though
I've got a long way still
There's no telling
Where I'd be
If it wasn't for you
Thinking of me

Chelsee BreAnn

It is Time to Leave

A heart
That has become
Empty
Filled with dust
Made from memories
Of the past
No more love
No one dares
Open the door
To the heart
They left vacant
Long before

Chelsee BreAnn

Here is Where You'll Stay

A heart
That has been
Loved
Filling up
What once was
Left empty
Only love
Only hope
Only dreams
From diamond minds
And crystal eyes
Love gleams

Chelsee BreAnn

Journey

Dreams of you
Wake me from sleep
And yet I sleep on and on
Healing is a journey
Time, a friend
But scars mark
My fragile skin
Is there a moment
When healing ends?

Self Care

You have cried enough tears
For a lifetime
It is time to allow yourself
To be happy

Chelsee BreAnn

I'm Proud of Me

They don't know the other part of me
The part that I've kept hidden for a while
The part I am ashamed of
. . . I *was* ashamed of
The feelings and emotions I have felt for a while now
But I've been too afraid to let show
I know now that the only way I can grow
Is to let people see me for who I am
I am not broken
I do not need "fixing"
Not mentally, not physically
I am me
And of that I have become proud

Survivor

I want to bring you back up
Like acid in my stomach
And pour you into
The pages of a book
So that everyone will know
That I am a survivor
I survived
You

Chelsee BreAnn

I Have Something to Say

My voice is loudest
When I'm writing

Labels for a Woman

What if you could see me now?
Thriving, like a blossoming flower
I needed the sunlight
But you only gave me shade
You kept me hidden from the world
When I needed the freedom to grow
Into the woman I am now
The woman you would call "rebellious"
"Unsubmissive," "unladylike"
But others call me "independent"
"Intelligent," brave"
And I call myself "fierce"
"Strong," "free"

Chelsee BreAnn

Gypsy Soul

My gypsy soul
A free-spirited being
Within me, it tries to break free
Waking in new light
Transforming into something that is whole
Something that is new
Something that has always been
Deep underneath the surface
Of my being
Of my skin
Arriving in just the right time
When I needed it to

Chelsee BreAnn

Happiness

Laying here
Listening to the conversation of raindrops
Mind drifting into deep thought
"I'm so happy"
A heart that was once broken and empty
Is now mended and full
All because of you
You make me happy

Chelsee BreAnn

Self Love

Things that I like:

I. Audrey Hepburn and her iconic lipstick

II. Poetry with meaning so deep it penetrates your soul before soaring to the stars

III. Lyrics written in such a way that make simple things have new meaning

IV. Cats

V. The way Mother Nature shines through my window each day to say "good morning," and sometimes just to say "you'll be ok"

VI. The way horses canter through fields believing they can fly

VII. Long walks to nowhere

VIII. The feel of a guitar under my fingers

IX. That rush of adrenaline right before I take the stage

X. Myself

Chelsee BreAnn

A Free Spirit

There is something so beautiful about a spirit that is free
It rides upon the wind as fiercely as an eagle
And lights upon the ground as tenderly as a feather

Chelsee BreAnn

To My Sister

Just look at what we made it through
A roller coaster of good days and bad
Most of them bad
Hitting rock bottom, then climbing our way
Back out of the canyon we fell into
Emerging even stronger than before
Ready to face the world

The moon shines on us now
And we shine right back
We create our own light
Now we know who we are
Invincible

Chelsee BreAnn

Acknowledgements

Thank you so much to those who have helped make my first book a reality. Thank you to my family and friends. Especially to my sister, Kimberly. They have been there for me during the toughest of times and have encouraged me to write. A big thank you to my boyfriend, Dexter, who is very supportive and the inspiration for many of my poems.

Thank you to Rebekah Ayres who did the artwork for my book. It truly captures the feel and emotion of my poetry. Also, to Raven Snow who did the lettering and made some adjustments to my book cover. Thank you to my alpha readers, Kimberly, Dylan, and Madelyn.

Lastly, thank you to those who support me on social media. You truly are inspirational and an encouragement. And to those who inspired my poetry, without you, I would have no story to tell and no lessons learned.

Chelsee BreAnn

Where can you find more of Chelsee BreAnn's poetry?

Books by Chelsee BreAnn:
Words, Poison and Love
Sugar Hearts and Candy Love

Books featuring Chelsee BreAnn:
Dark Thirty Poetry Anthology One

You can also follow Chelsee on Instagram @chelseebreannpoet

Please leave me a review on Amazon and Goodreads!

Chelsee BreAnn

Index

Chelsee BreAnn

www.ingramcontent.com/pod-product-compliance
Lightning Source LLC
Chambersburg PA
CBHW060318050426

42449CB00011B/2541